Shelby's

Christmas Surprise

To
To Lana and Lea
Love You Forever

Meet Shelby, a curious and playful Snowshoe kitten.

Once upon a time...

In a cozy little town, a snowshoe kitten named Shelby fell from the school roof right in front of a girl named Lana.

She scooped him up and brought him home.

From that day, Shelby became a beloved part of her family.

However, Lana's little sister Lea jumped in and said "Shelby is my cat!"

Shelby loved his new home. He was a playful kitten with bright blue eyes and a mischief in his whiskers. The little guy bounced around the house every day, always ready to play with anyone who would join him.

He was always up to something. He climbed on shelves, tore at curtains, and even tried to eat food from the table!

However, the family's Bengal cat, Leona and their fluffy white Pomeranian dog named Giggi were not very ready for Shelby mischief

"Oh, there goes wild kitten again!" sighed Leona.

Shelby would leap onto her back, tap her gently, and then race away. Giggi just yawned and looked up while Shelby pounced after her tail, playfully.

One day, Shelby felt bored because no one wanted to play with him.

He knew Christmas was coming, and he wanted to find the perfect way to make Lana and Lea happy.

And then in a flash he thought of something. "I'm a snowshoe cat, and what do snowshoes need? Socks! I'll be the best Christmas gift ever! Shelby thought proudly.

The only thing was, he needed a set of Christmas stockings first.

Off he went, pawing through drawers and knocking over stacks of cozy socks. But none were Christmassy enough for Shelby

Then, he spotted the stockings by the fireplace – bright red, fluffy, and filled with candy.

He jumped to grab a stocking.

Shelby pushed the candies aside
to wiggle his way inside.

Just as he got cozy, his little face peeked out, and at that very moment, Lea, noticed him.

"Look, Mom!" said Lea. "We got a gift for Christmas – our charming prince Shelby!"

That night, everyone gathered around to hug and kiss Shelby, making him feel proud to be so smart, beautiful, and loved. It was the best Christmas ever!

The End

Merry Christmas

and Thank You for Reading

Made in United States
Troutdale, OR
11/28/2024

25427898R00017